Self Hate

African American Churches Stimulating the Issues that Come Along with Self Hate

CHARLES THOMAS

First published by Dog Ear Publishing
4010 W. 86th Street, Ste H
Indianapolis, IN 46268
www.dogearpublishing.net

ISBN: 978-1-4575-2613-8

This book is printed on acid-free paper.

Printed in the United States of America

ACKNOWLEGDEMENTS

This book will be dedicated because of my understanding of the teaching of the late W.D. Muhammad, and the knowledge he has for mankind, because of my study and his universal knowledge of the spiritual insights of the revelation, of the words of truth and the paths of truth that a person must walk. You see one can only get this insight! if you are invited and a seeker of the truth, and you have to seek it and work with and open heart by the spirit of this truth, this is only my testimonial and what I got from his lecturers and DVD's and booklets, on so many levels, and his righteousness of truth and the love that he had for the lost people of this new world (and the old world of Egypt), and his love of his mother and his father and his family that he never sold us out! He has always been true to enlighten the world with the truth about who we are as a people. He not only told you, but he also told the whole world of your conditions, and what the solutions are for your recovery.

With the unconditional love and faith that he had for the black man today also our ancestors of the past, and his love for mankind alike, here in the land of North America and around the world of mankind, I asked that Allah (the covenant) would forgive him of his sins and grant him paradise among the other great leader of our times past and the present and the future. Then bless everything that was put in his heart that he started while he was with us, and the fact that I was blessed to have the understanding to hear his knowledge and apply it to this life, and may it grow forever more. And the great seed that he planted in the mines for spiritual leverage, and freedom for mankind and his people the lost and found tribe of African American's hear in the lands of North America.

CHAPTER 1

(NO ONE LIKE A LOAFER, NOT EVEN A LOAFER)

*T*his book is dedicated to mankind and African Americans and to the opening of the spiritual side of our souls, and of our mine's to the understanding of self- hate, the target and tragedy's, for the subject is the African American's communities! And just what the African American black churches are doing, or not doing for the community's. And also how self- hate has become a part of African American way of life and our cultural paradigm, and it is a very paradoxical problem, and the misleading of the leadership in the African American families, then to our moral sins as a people, and may we be forgiven of our sins that we have inflicted on ourselves as a people. Because I think this is what you need to know as a people, that we have reduced ourselves morally to its lowest form as a human family and a people we have adapted to this darkness because this is all we know, because down here where we live as a people there is only artificial light (truth) not natural light (truth). You see there is only mans truth and the creator's truth. And we have taken on ourselves what man said we are not what the creator created us as.

Now which one of these truths will keep you in the darkness? And let me say this no one wants to be in the condition that we have been condition for as a people, and no one else can help you but yourself, and only the creator can remove us from these depths of artificial truths, and you were stolen and put hear by men (you are the bottom rail) and that only with love can you elevate yourself with the help of the Covenant understanding. You can become that new people only if you operate within the Covenant of Peace. African American people has to know the different between Christianity and antichrist because what the African American preacher's are teaching us as a people is a crime against humanity we have to be educated on how to love yourselves before you teach African American to love another man's image, And to know the horror's and the side effects of breaking the second commandment about the worship of a image and how this doctrine is propagated still among the communities we need to learn how to work together as a people and feel and become proactive with economics and stop giving all of our wealth away because of the self-hate of worshipping the image of another man and you can love yourselves enough to do something for the future for you own family NO ONE LIKES A LOAFER.

Another thing that enters into play is that fact that we as a people have been self conditioning ourselves! with the worshipping of the image of another man as our G_D and rejecting ourselves or even the denying oneself as a people to want a better community future for the next generations that are yet to be born. And what is being given in the African American community's though the Black church's is only a self conditioning teaching that our ancestors used to get and there is no growth in this conditioning for working together as a community for our future generations This is not hate talk, it is help talk. And you must learn the different and step out side of your condition and see that you are the problem and take ownership of the correction that needs to take places within you and the communities. Because the same problem is in every African American neighborhood across this great country and your future depends on us developing self belief in us as a people. We have to learn how to part the waters of faith, as MOSE did with the people of Israel.

And the process that the Pharaoh used on the children of Israel and anti Israel can bring a people to this deadly demise, and any people who will reduce another people to this level (WHITE AMERICA) that will keep a people blind, deaf and Dum and dysfunctional, and we still think enough of them to worship their image as our LORDS and Savior and we get bent out of shape when they don't give you something that you could have gotten yourself, if you love yourself and work together and stop acting like you are not important, this is what the black preacher has reduced us to self-hate and self-conditioning. When you read the bible and you get drilled every week that you are the least and we still care about the black preachers and their feelings, and have a great respect for their accomplishments and we still walk and talk and work as if you have no problem with the way in which you have been treated, and you are okay with that and want only the scraps that fall from the rich man's table which is very little in return, you are a great people. But take a close look at what the black churches have done to us for over four hundred years! And then ask yourselves who needs a huge; somebody has broken the Covenant of peace just like the children of Israel did. And we are a people that have been broke into little pieces, we have the Hump Te Dump Te virus.

Just because you and I cannot change the past, and for you to understand as African Americans that the past is something that our creator has put us thought! He just wanted to show the world that he can cause death to a people and that he can raise a people out of that death. Or roll that stone away from that tome of darkness and let the light of truth shine into that darkness. Only to show mankind how important his Covenant is and that death come on his created man when the Covenant that he designed for mankind is broken, and how far man can go into sin. And that the only way for mankind to return to his created self! Is too purge himself back though his spiritual Covenant and to MORALLY correct himself and that Son of Man can raise from the grave of the dead and return to his chosen created life. Now this is what the study and the teaching of the late W.D. Muhammad has open up my eyes to the understanding of the last Covenant and it is called ALLAH, I was a student of his, and I studied his language.

If you don't know any better you can't do any better. Then the Worshipping of the image of them as our G_D and for them to teach us that they dead for the sin of the world and everybody has to go and worship this image of him for eternal life, and then we share everything with them. Now I am going to tell you something that you have never heard before but it is your truth, you can take it or leave it but it will not change this fact.

This is what a NIGGER is in case you didn't know, and this is why the word NIGGER hurts us as deeply as a people, only a NIGGER would worship another man as his G_D. And it will take another Nigger to feel the pain and suffering of this state of mine, the pain run's deep from generation to generation because the Black so called Preachers is still keeping us in a Nigger state of mine yes, Nigger it is a condition, it is like being unconscious, I don't care how much education you have, and I don't care how many movies you have star in, or how well you played the game of sports even if you become the President of whatever we all as African American have had that Nigger conditioning and we can't get free of this condition because it is told over and over every Sunday morning by the black preachers to stay a NIGGER and worship this white man image as your G_D and thank him for everything he has done for you and he the Black preacher will continue to give him your tides and offering away. The black Preachers yes him! he just takes and takes and don't give back. I would like to say this and it would be the truth! That our 10 % would go further if the Black communities could use that great 10% before it goes back out of the African American communities. That every SUNDAY! Across this USA that MILLIONS of dollars that come out of black Churches and goes to the G_D that they worship, the white IMAGE, I started to name this book (WHAT IS A NIGGER) or better yet (NIGGER PLEASE) what is a NIGGER? And don't get what I am saying twisted, this is not hate talk it is truth talk. Know the truth and it will set you free! And don't hate the message; you have to work together and help one another you can't put new wine in an old bag. The way the African American churches our working they will not get us as a people where we need to be as a people if they continue to stay divide against one another as denominations under the Image of another man as G_D. that will not cut it anymore.

Now this is the new wine that will raise your spirit. We love Jesus because he was treated like a NIGGER, he was a good man that believed in his people the poor and only wanted them to know that the Covenant was the promise for everyone it has no seams, it is like the SUN it will shine on the good and the bad, and like the earth it don't care what seed you plant in it, it is created to grow whatever the seed is, and water don't care who drinks it, it has a Covenant within it to give life and substance it. Your mine works the same way with your thoughts can manifest

6

into something real. And because the poor was made poor by the hand of man and man wanted to keep his control over man just like the black preacher in our community's want to keep control over our future so they let the Romans laws hanged him and stopped his dream. We don't need to know anything else about JESUS! Other thin the fact his life was all about his Covenant, so they the community leaders turned on him and the message of the truth to HANG him to silence him.

Well that is the Black preachers and persons that is of your kind in color and cultural conditioning, which will teach another persons of color for generations after generations that he will never be as good as this white person on the cross, which I am telling you to worship as your G_D. And that his death is the greatest death that any man can do for mankind. (Now that was the old wine,) And then that NIGGRO (preacher) will tell you that is the only way too Heaven is through him and for you to go out and make another NIGGER with what I teach you about what this great white man has done for you and other NIGGER'S like yourself and bring them to church with you next time and I will teach them the same story.

They are the sinners if they don't come to some church and listen to what we NIGGRO preachers are saying. So we can take more money out of our community's and build more large church's to serve this white G_D. and keep the African American community divided that they will not know the truth! If it get right in our faces. Now how sick is that, this is a crime against humanity and it needs to be addressed legally, this is the reason that we have to deal with all of this self-hate. And the black family's are broken, and the young man are in prisons, we disrespect our women, all of these problems come from and are a side effect of not believing in the Covenant, and not believing in ourselves, and not doing for ourselves.

And for you Black man to teach us to turn your back on your future generations, the white G_D image is more important than your future. What I see is that the black preacher has created, is a turn the other cheek people, We turn the other cheek when it come to the Covenant belief, we turn the other cheek when it come to belief in yourselves, we turn the cheek when it comes to doing something for self, and we turn the other cheek when it come to respecting are family's, and we really turn the other cheek when it comes to building a future for our children, we also turn the other cheek when it comes to respecting another man wife or family, Hell the church has just made us a turn the other cheek people. Look at all of this life that has past us a people! And we have turned the other cheek on time as a people.

And the time we have spent doing nothing but turning the other cheek and giving the community's wealth away to these jack leg preacher that have only been educated on taking your wealth and oppressing the community's advancements' of community life in the name of religion, and not discussing the important of the Covenant of love, and peace, and working together as one people, under this one Covenant that other Prophets educated their people about. No this uneducated black preacher wants you under religion to rob you of a future and community life. Will a man ROB G_D how he will still your future and soul also.

Now this is self- hate and white supremacy at its apex if you agree or don't agree it will not change this fact. And that is what a NIGGER (preacher) will tell you and we in turn teach our children to be a NIGGER and you give them transferred self-hate and white supremacy to the next generation because this is what your parents did to you! So to you it must be right because everyone is carrying that NIGGER weight of self-hate and the NIGGER (Preachers) is giving all of our hard earned money away in your tides and offering. How can a man rob G_D! If he gets you to break the COVENANT you are in a NIGGER state of mine. Like the children of Israel they worshipped Pharaoh this is the same condition that MOSES had to work with, but the only different is we only worship the white man image as G_D. So white America has done to us what the Pharaohs have done to the children of Israel you educated preachers.

And we have to stand up on our own two feet as a people, and stop being a drag on the society's that we our living in and grow up as a people, yes just like the dry bones of the Bible! We have the manual if you would only teach the real meaning of this manual! If you cannot understand it from the correct prospective of the covenant then I suggest that you stop teaching the black man to turn the other cheek, and teach him how to stand up and get some community life as tough people (we have only the power to change what is in us, not the power to change what is in another man heart)! Only the creator of that other man he has to change his self, we Mr. black have the power to stop the self hate

If it wasn't the truth! My parents would not have done this to me because they loved us, but the power of a lie that is told long enough will not change the fact that it was created to break the COVENANT and get you out of its protection of his promise. And he will want you to give everything you have to this G_D or white Image. (Pharaohs had the same problem he created a lot of self-hate he made himself as a G_D to Israel) and keep nothing for yourself now he the NIGGER (preachers) is teaching you to be a NIGGER! Too not want for yourself and don't do for yourself. For you to hate being black, because you can't change who you are! this NIGGERO PREACHER wants you to stay in a poor spirit and a poor condition because that is your lot in life. And he can give your tide and offering away to his G_D, because his G_D will take and bless and multiply your tide and offering then he will get a kick back for creating the most NIGGERS and it's because you are NIGGERS and you act like NIGGERS, (So NIGGER) is a state of MINE and the black Preacher's are keeping that state of mine open to self-hate his G_D is white that he prays too and he will stand in front of you and tell you this lie every Sunday and at Bible study mid week. Then we can go hungry and teach our children not to want a future for their self, just enjoy what another man gives you because he is your G_D, and you black man just keep being that NIGGER I made you a NIGGER we can keep on stealing from one another! Then we keep on killing one another, and we keep on disrespecting our woman, and he can keep giving our ten percent away with no return on that ten percent. And we let are young man go in and out of prison without support of community and fathers having no respect for family life because the preacher is stealing your future and he is also robbing the creator of his created people, and the teaching of a false Doctrine that is causing self-hate.

Now you know what a NIGGER! Is and how you where put into this condition and how you were kept in this condition this Is how to make another NIGGER! And how we teach our children to become a NIGGER people! And we take a back seat to being a responsible man to our manhood and we leave our family and our community's in lawlessness and our children are unprotected and we teach our young woman that men only want one thing because we didn't respect our woman! And how we enjoyed this life that the black preachers have created for us to turn the cheek on community life, and turn the cheek on family life and turn the cheek on our children future, as a NIGGER, This is what you are born into but you don't have to stay in this condition and not believing in yourself and stop giving everything that the churches have collected back to another community but learn how to use the money in your family and community! Before you let it go out of your community's you

have always gave and not keep anything for your future generations. Don't let the preacher keep making you stay in this condition of his created NIGGER ; you see he is like the witch
Doctor that will get you spell bound and ask you to put your
faith into and object that can't help you. But the only object that
can get us to stand as a community you have to start to live for
the future of self and stop all the self-hate. So when someone
calls you a NIGGER, just say to that person soon and very soon
I will be out of that condition or mine set, now that I know
more about my condition I can start the process of change and
now, But the important thing is that you know that we have
done this to ourselves! And it can be reversed.

Stop giving away your tides and offering NIGGER (Preachers) put it away for a rainy day and get a return on your invest-
ment and stop making more NIGGERS. Teach us to believe in
ourselves and use the tide and offering in your communities
before you give the tide and offering back to your G_D. Take
control of your family's, take control of your education, take
control of your communities, take control of your morals,
believing in self. This is what we look like to other nation and
cultures we need a fix of self and get pass this hate of self.

But we must let the grand children of the slave master know
what their grandfather and mothers did to make us turn on one
another and to this date it is still working and it is the cause of
our self- hate. I am not trying to cause more hate but to clear the
air and level the playing field, and give more understanding of

white supremacy and why they burn the cross and we fear the cross, so we as mankind and as a people can go on with our lives, just let them know the hell that we are in because they need to know that they their grandparents did this to you as a people! and don't forget your ancestors, that give their life for a better day and their needs for us to be independent, and to govern ourselves and to position our souls for freedom peace and justice and equality, and how many give their life for this cause and purpose , because we are in a dark place in our spirit and or mines and separated from are spiritual journey of faith. To protect one another especially the mothers of our children's because if she is not protected then or families are not protected, then MORALS become a problem and we have to stop playing these games of self- hate on one another and get real about are future and start building for our next generations collectively. We black we complain the most and we do the least to change our condition because we have been educated to not believe in yourselves but to believe in another IMAGE and we brake our own spirit of self love, too make that Image first in our life's and you can't serve two masters so we brake that covenant of the PROPHET of old, just to worship the image and make another man image your G_D. And we get behind close door and talk about how we hate the white man, but we like everything about him and what he makes and we have him on every wall of our homes and in every place of worship. Then on top of all that the Bible teaches you not to worship the image of any man, but you do? You tell me who is right and who is wrong, is the Bible a lie or are you condition to believe a lie. (You got to tell the truth, and do the truth, and if you care you will live the truth).

We have to ask ourselves just what is it that our African American spiritual leaders hope to gain with them teaching us the worship of another man as our G_D and not loving yourself first and doing for yourself first. I see this as the seed of self-hate, just look at your BIBLE your TORAH and QURAN! They convey the same message of how one man over powers another, and forces himself on the man with fears. And what if those fears (where symbolic and used as Lions as in the story Daniel in the lion den, and the lions where something that can devour you like a lion) like self-hate and also that is over powering too force the worship of this Image of a man as G_DS or to fear his image as being the creator of the heavens and the owner of the day of judgment. I don't take this lightly; this statement is for mankind to understand his position when the hammer falls on the leadership in the African American Community's.

We have had a polar shift, mentally and spiritually; this has damaged our power to work together for our future. And no other people has every been keep and forced into this kind of darkness, and deeply caste down into this kind of hell whole (relating to duration or extent), of self- hate for as long as we have as a people, and too see that people wanted to be satisfied with the conditions of hell and will get MAD if you try and change the condition of not worshipping the image of another man, or make them aware of the condition or show them they are in the condition of self-hate, and they not wanting away out, of this darkness but only you and I know what life is like in this kind of darkness. (This is the same kind of well or condition that Joseph was put in and he also was sold into slavery by his bothers) but he like JOB keep the faith, if you remember he wanted a way out he told the two men to remember him before the King.

Other people need to know what their ancestors (White America) put on us as a people, and the long term affects of the evil spirit of self- hate, and the whole subject has nothing to do with keeping more hate in your face because I want to remove it from our culture as a people but to know it is a driving force with black on black crime. Only the hate of what we have become, because of the deep level of slavery that we had to endure as a people, because we our ancestors broke the Covenant of LIFE CREATEDNESS this has caused us as a people not to believe in ourselves, but we have also adopted another man's indoctrination of his percept of what G_D is, this indoctrination has us living in a state of undeveloped and then to live in a unconscious state of mine as a people that this condition has produced, and we as a people have succumb to this deep condition of self hate! And it is no one blame it is the fact, that we as a people are out of the Covenant and it has put us as a people in this condition, and the only way out of this condition is back through the Covenant of ADAM it has not changed.

As a result of it we need to have a circumcision performed by the Covenant of ALLAH (ADAM). He is the only light of truth that can lift self hate form the spirit of man, and forgive our ancestors of false worship of a man's image but you have to want it to be removed and conduct yourselves as if you want it removed, then to know that this self hate has the whole world of mankind at its worse. That this is not what the CREATOR had planned for his created being mankind, was all of this self hate. We all have the same enmity! And I am not trying to give him anymore power; by creating more hate I just want Africa American's to know that it is time to be more responsible for his and hers action and MAN UP and WOMAN UP! to his family life and community life and prepare for your own future as a people, and stop blaming other people for our LAZYNESS and the self hate, be more ashamed of being exploited for the rest of our generational future's. You are a free people so just start acting like you are free we have all we need to become productive with love and respect.

The fact is clear that this is an internal problem that we have, because we are educated in are places of worship not to believe in ourselves and to do nothing for our community life and the future generations. That we have made gossip and putting one another down and undermining each other seem normal, this is one reason we have so many denominations of religion because deep in your heart you know religion is manmade, and we don't understand the keys of the parabolic language of G_DS words and we try and take it for its face value.

This is the seed of our death as a people, not to want your own freedom of responsibility's to govern your own future. And then why wouldn't an African American people want to do for himself unless he has been condition to hates himself because his brother the black pastor has programmed us not to want a future for yourselves, why else would a person drink himself to death, or to drug himself to death, or walk away from his family life or abuse the mother of his children I THANK! that we have to overcome a lot of our immoral and our inhuman differences, and I 'am speaking as a black man with years of experience of self hate, I can and I 'am willing to change my views on the control of myself hate, and turn it into self respect, I know other nationality's can consider this fact also about the conditioning of self hate, that seem to come to different culture. Then and only then when we instill these values of self respect in our family's first! Because it has to start their first; This is the change that has to start on the inside and work it way out first, Like the prophet Jesus said and(may the peace and blessing of the Covenant be on him) we have to be born again into the right spirit, and then let that new spirit of joy that comes from being free of self hate, Then individuals go among ourselves and show and live for the love of that change that goes out to the ones that are close's to us as family's and kin folk, love your neighbors as you love yourselves and then members of others cultures. But serve yourself first give yourselves ten percent of self respect like money, it will begin to compound your faith in one another and as it grows increase it to twenty percent and the goal is to get it up to one hundred percent..

Then it will spread to their family's next door and run down the streets of the cities, and into the Governments and the hearts of the people your cup will run over. That action will feed this new spirit of love, which has purged us and made us free of self hate, because when you have someone that thinks they are better than anyone else and they make a image of themselves as G_D. they are saying that G_D loves them more than any of you. (Now that is what Pharaohs did he made himself as a G_D) Well that person has sure come to self hate again and that person is putting his self in a position to be harmed, or has put someone else that is close to him and the problem is this. And we don't know the depth of the sin and the pain or how long it will last, or the damage that will come to those that he love, and or that harm don't care what color you are or how good you look or how much you love him or her or that child's age or how long you been Married and so on and so forth, you always pay for your action one way or another, you create what you are dealt by our own action and deeds. And you should be careful with the company that you keep. Just look at what it has done to US as a people! The Key word in this chapter is OBEDIENCE not for self but for the body of people that are willing to make a change, those that want to do right and all the pain of our ancestor, and the ones that don't know that there is a right way. Because we all have the same enemy SELF HATE! And it will not go away on its own, there has to be a collective generative that has to be afforded. For those of you that think they have a understanding of the Bible well it is a book that was sent to us at this time period to see this perspectives of a timeline and show us how many time that Religion has gotten in the way of mankind growth and he has to send a messenger or a prophet to straighten mankind back to the path and out of self hate. Because he mankind has lost his way and begins to worship other G_D now if I am wrong tell me.

You have to know that self hate will destroy you from the inside out; it is a force that once it is set in motion (state of mine) it will stay in motion until acted upon by an opposite and equal motion. Hate is not a gift from the creator mankind but from the enemy of mankind, it only feeds of the hate that we create and it has grown to be a monster that is how well we have been feeding it. If you stop feeding it then it will die of no food right. Hate it is not of you! It can and will do damage it can spreads to someone that is close to you or put something in your path that will block a future blessing that will be connected to something that you prayed for. Then it may hold that blessing from coming to its fullest potential and arrive to you or someone else undeveloped or premature. And the same blessing can be for a people or a person or a Government and a nation. What you must condition your selves to the fact that we have to stop thinking as individuals and purge ourselves of this self hate that lives and is ingrained in the fibers of our life, and cast it out into the pit of hell from where it came. So that we can live as other society, and with the respect that is needed as a people

CHARLES THOMAS

that have freed themselves from self hatred and not to let other people stop the progress of that much needed change for us as people and don't get puffed up with proud because proud is another killer.

You know the word is what the world was created with so let us surround ourselves with the words of that truth and create this world that we so much need, and stop all of this self hatred and practice what we preach as it was said to us by Jesus (that we walk by faith not by sight) don't let the glitter of this world blind you. WE HAVE TO HAVE FAITH IN HIS Covenant! And get what you need for a good and desirable community life. If you don't practice what you preach' then you are saying that you hate what has been created for you to be what G_D wants us to be and deny the truth that has been preached to you. So you end up fooling yourselves because you can't fool the LAWS of the Covenant it is wrote in blood and will not change.

A great example of self hate from the Jewish Book; the TANAKH and from the chapter of Jeremiah 42, It is about a people that is free and was full of fear! Then all the army offices, with Johanan son of Kareah Jezaniah son of Hoshaiah, and all the rest of the people, great and small, approached the prophet Jeremiah and said, Grant our plea, and pray for us to the Lord your G_D, for all this remnant, For we remain but, a few out of many, as you can see. Let the Lord your G_D tell us where we should go and what we should do.

20

The prophet Jeremiah answered them "Agreed: I will pray to the Lord your G_D as you request, and I will tell you whatever response the Lord gives for you. I will withhold nothing from you."Thereupon they said to Jeremiah; Let the Lord be a true and faithful witness against us! We swear that we will do exactly as the Lord your G_D instructs us through you Whether it is pleasant or unpleasant we will obey the Lord our G_D to whom we send you, in order that it may go well with us when we obey the Lord our G_D.

After ten days, the word of the Lord came to Jeremiah. He called Johanan son of Kareah and all the army officers, and the rest of the people great and small, and said to them, "Thus said the Lord, the G_D of Israel (the Covenant), to whom you sent me to resent your supplication before Him: If you remain in this land, I will build you and not overthrow, I will plant you and not uproot; for I regret the punishment I have brought upon you. Don't be afraid of him declares the Lord for I am with you to save you and to rescue you from his hands. I will dispose him to be merciful to you: he shall show you mercy and bring you back to your own land.

But if you say, we will not stay in this land thus disobeying the Lord Your G_D (the Covenant) if you say, No! We will go to the land of Egypt, so that we may not see war or hear the sound of the horn and so that we may not hunger for bread; there we will stay, then hear the word of the Lord, O remnant of Judah! Thus said the Lord of Host (the covenant)' the G_D of Israel: If you turn your faces toward Egypt, and you go and sojourn there, the land sword that you fear shall overtake you there, in the land of Egypt; and the famine you worry over shall follow at your heels in Egypt, too; and there you shall die. All the men who turn their faces toward Egypt, in order to sojourn there, shall die by the sword, by famine, and by pestilence. They shell have no surviving remnant of the disaster that I will bring upon them For thus said the Lord of Hosts,(the covenant)the G_D of Israel As my anger and wrath were poured out upon the inhabitants of Jerusalem, so will my wrath be poured out on you if you go to Egypt. You shall become an execration of woe, a curse and a mockery; and you shall never again see this place. The Lord has spoken against you, O remnant of Judah! Do not go to Egypt! Know well, then for I warn you this day that you were deceitful at heart when you sent me to the lord your G_D, saying, pray for us to the Lord our G_D; and whatever the Lord our G_D may say, just tell us and we will do it. I told you today, and you have not obeyed the Lord your G_D in respect to all that he sent me to tell you know well, then that you shall die by the sword, by famine, and by pestilence in the place where you to go and sojourn.

Now what you just read is a perfect example of what mankind does and, just to get himself into disobedience with his creator, because of his free will. But there is free will under his Covenant also. But mankind always and in most of the stories of the word of G_D man has look the other way when it comes to the obedience to the Covenant. Now remember the number one commandment of the Covenant is.

1. Thou shall have no other G_D before me!

2. Thou shall not make unto thee any graven image!

We as mankind the human family cannot keep these first two commands. And let me make the statement now if the people of Jeremiah, they even told him to pray to the Lord (the Covenant) and whatever he tell Jeremiah and he Jeremiah give them the good and the bad, and they choice the bad because of their lack of faith. They will do what most people of the books of G_D do and because of fear make the wrong choice! But they didn't listen to what G_D told them. Then G_D always tell us what the consequences of their and our action will be, even at the time of Jesus. They the people where asked which person shall we release or set free and we choice the rebellious one Barabbas, not the one that preformed many miracle. We made that choice base on the religion leader at that time. Because we have fear of man and not G_D! I can't help but to feel that the religious leader had a hand in convincing the people to make the wrong choice. Because he Jesus didn't like or didn't agree with the program that was given to the people! (Jewish) or (righteous) he Jesus had a whole new Message that was from the blood line of Adam, Abraham, Jacob, and Moses Muhammad That new message was mankind has forgotten about the (Covenant) and was under the fear of that culture of Rome, and the controlling Jewish leaders of man. Now we find the need for the same kind of a fix that the Jewish people at the time of Jesus was in but they are preachers doing the rejection of righteousness not the Rabbi's, and hear again and the fix has not changed sense Genesis to Revelation it Is the understanding of the Covenant that is the fix. Not anything else can help mankind out the mess that he has created. We have to stand on the promise of (the Covenant) it will never change.

Deuteronomy Chapter 30 1:5

1. And it shall come to pass, when all these things are come upon thee. The blessing and the curse, which I have set before thee.(which means Mankind must choice the way of the Covenant, and not of fear) and thou shall call them to mind among all the nations, whither the Lord (the Covenant) thy G_D hath driven thee.

2. And shall return unto the Lord (the Covenant) thy G_D, and shall obey his voice according to all that I command (commandments of the Covenant) thee this day, thou and thy children. With all thy heart and with all thy soul;

3. That then the Lord (the Covenant) thy G_D will turn thy captivity (which is those that are out of the covenant) and have compassion upon thee, and will

return and gather thee from all the nations, whither the Lord (the Covenant) thy G_D hath scattered thee.

4. If any of thee be driven out unto the outmost parts of heaven, from thence will the Lord (the Covenant) thy G_D gather thee, and from thence will he fetch thee.

5. And the Lord (the Covenant) thy G_D will bring thee into the land which thy fathers possessed, and thou shall possess it; and he will do thy good, and multiply thee above thy fathers.

You have to see yourselves as a people in this book, dark skinned people! You are the ones lacking in your needs as a people of self hate and are totally out of the will of your Lord (the Covenant) thy G_D, get out of the box of self hate, and take a good look at the worshipping of the Image of another man.

CHAPTER 2

As Long As I am In the World, I am the Light of the World

*W*e need to move closer to the understanding of (the Covenant) of ALLAH (Quran SURAH 2 AYAT 27) and (Quran SURAH I4 AYAT 1) in order to get close to your created self and on the path of human righteousness, it has been said to us time and time again but what stop us or pollute us and hold us back is all of these different religions or denominations, it is that false creation of man, self hate it will cause self dough and the lack of faith, it will cause lose of self control, you lose direction and It will cause the growth of selfishness, individualism It will destroy family's it will destroy city's it will destroy nation's It will destroy creation it has destroyed the Blackman.

Now from a legal prospective just take a look at this, how many times have we destroyed the future of some white company or someone's white's reputation just because they say the word NIGGER at the wrong time or you think it is out of order and unwanted! And on the other hand you go to a church in the black community and he the black preacher teach you that the white man is your G_D after all the books on spirituality you read tells you not to worship any images and for you to love yourself! Because he, the creator said so and he put this in writing. And you get bent out of shape when someone calls you a NIGGER but this BLACK PREACHER is keeping us in this NIGGER condition and tell you that this image is what you need to have eternal life, but don't let him call you a NIGGER if he does this then go after him legally and the NAACP and other black organizations with a Christian base leadership as its head! We will support your fight for your rights. And you know that this black preacher is doing you wrong and he is stealing your future and giving your future and your ten percent away so the Real creator will not bless you because we have no faith in black people and you will not teach about how to operate under the promise of the HOLY COVENANT! But he gives you self hate. This is what the Black Preacher is telling the Negros in the black church under the leader ship of the indoctrination of the adopted religion. It is not the word NIGGER that make you upset it is the condition that the BLACK preachers will not help you escape from economically. So when someone calls you the "N" word if you want to get mad at someone then turn on the black preacher because he is the keeper of the condition of the "N" word alive for a pat on the head from the white man. Now this statement is not about hating any person! It about hates the condition of the black community's and the African American community getting a bad rape because of the greed and the selfishness of other's.

Self-hate it will destroy the environments that give us life, it will cause nation to turn on one another or on each other on the small level or large even us. If you want to destroy a people just tell them long enough that they are nothing and never will be nothing and reducing them to nothing keeps them uneducated and poor and then they are self contained or they have imprisoned themselves, and if they want to try and be somebody and have something for himself and you continue just keep telling them or him that this is what you will only be and nothing else. It will cause that people or person to have no faith or become spiritually blind and a deep sleep will overtake them and the condition of self hate to fall upon a people or a nation and they will be wrapped in that condition until someone removes that stone from their grave or the cave. So the light of truth comes in to free them, and that light it represents the light of truth. If no truth comes it will cause all of Mankind to fall deeper into the sin of self Hate. I have to look at white America and how with their power and drive to control the world and that they made an image of themselves as a G_D or the Lord that has die for the World sins and if you believe in the Image of them as G_D you will be saved. (Well read this if you where to change the image of G_D to a black image all African Americans would stop going to church because of the self hate that we have for ourselves thanks to the black preacher's).

And that the world may live if they the Humans or Mankind follow their ways of life! That man will live because of this image. Now even if you believe that and it is totally up to you, I don't care! But you must see that if you are not a White person how this is teaching other's that are nonwhite it promote self hate, WHY IS THAT! Because you are not in that blood line. So you feel that you are not a part of that bloodline and not one of the inheritor and you are treated like and orphaned. So you feel obligated to give everything to this image or anything that looks like that image NOW LIKE I SAID! If you feel comfortable with that then just keep on keeping on, but don't tell me how much you hate the Whiteman or you hate the problem in the black community's poverty and you try to tell me that white people did this and white folks that, you need not read any more and think you for your time.

But if you can see that self hate and my believing in the image of a white Jesus and that it is a cause of self hate and you want to know more stay with the language and study the teaching of W.D. Mohammed and read your BIBLE with your heart not just your eyes. Now because we are not white! As the Image of G_D that is portrayed in Christianity we are told over and over, that G_D love you but you see that he love one people more then he love you, and you begin to question G_D because you know that G_D love everybody and I am here to tell you that the self hate that we have been submerged in and artificially religion and we our simulated into their culture and personality. This is a flag that show us that we have a great hate for each other, and don't that tell us that the worshipping of another man and of another blood line has created this hidden self hatred that is running all around in the black community all over the world. There is no greater sin that can be committed against G_D, just look at what happen to Egypt's Pharaohs who's clams that they were G_Ds! Open up your hearts people, the wages of sin is death, not a physical death but a spiritual death or being spiritually blind to this truth of the Covenant.

Now what comes to mine is the fact that the Bible say for MAN! is Not to make any graven images and or the worship of anything in creation, and in the oceans or anything of the Heavens. Now if this comes about and you follow this path of believes in the worship of anything that he created, why because there is only one creator and only one Covenant, that has come to mankind with different names which changed for different time periods! but it is the same Covenant to follow for his creatures. Then for you to get side tracked and worship the image of another created man as your Lord and savior.

Then you are condition by that same people to drink his blood and to eat his flesh, and to love him that image more then you love yourself. Well my people that's how we got in this self hate conditioning, the worse part of this is that you have no protection of the promise of the Covenant, you're naked and alone. You can't produce the spirit that come from living the disciple life of the COVENANT their isn't a religion to replace it or substitute the power of it. You can't hurt the creator he can make another man to replace you. If you break the Covenant of the creator you can return to the Covenant if you purge yourselves of what caused you to break the Covenant which is the worshipping of a false image and self hate. Then you know that this is the only thing that matter in his creation, is your obedience to pray in the Discipline of his Covenant and return back to your original self! If you recall Mary she was a virgin of the spirit of the COVENANT she had no other man or religion and because of her purity she give birth to pure spirit of the prophet Jesus you have to understand this blood line of the HOLY COVENANT it has always been right in your face on the page of his word it is a COVENANT of peace and balance of the human spirit and it is maintain with praying to the COVENANT.

Now do not thank you can get around this fact without a punishment. But one fact that you should know and believe me it is a good reason to want to change, from this self hate! Because you can't grow as a spiritual person or as a spiritual leader as long as you hold onto this self hate. You can't grow as a family or you can't as a community and you can't grow as a nation any longer because of self hate and your enemy will keep you in fear of not having the keys to using your faith. You are at a disadvantage and you are expected to stay in that position until someone comes alone and save's you and you have to want to be saved.

Now something that you don't know is this and you can thank your ancestors for this, because they give you the TORAH to make you aware of the problem that you will face in this time period because that false doctrine of religion has swallowed you like the great fish? Or religion it is riding you like you are a donkey (unintelligent person). Or it is what caused JOB to lose everything, and ADAM to be cast out of the garden! self hate the evil one told him that he could be more or like G_D, he wanted to be more, and didn't like what G_D had given him wasn't enough mankind is never satisfied.

Psalm 115 1:18

1. Not unto us, O lord (the Covenant), not unto us, but unto thy name give glory, for thy mercy, and for thy truths sake.

2. Wherefore should the heathen say where their G_D is now?

3. But our G_D is in the heavens: (you see him in his creation) he has done whatsoever he hath pleased.

4. Their idols are silver and gold, the work of men's hands.

5. They have mouths, but they speck not: eyes have they, but they see not.

6. They have ears, but they hear not: noses have they, but they smell not.

7. They have hands, but they handle not: feet have they, but they walk not: neither speck they through their throat.

8. <u>They that make them are like unto them</u>; (now just look at the image of Jesus what feature does he has) so is every one that trust in them.

9. O Israel, trust thou in the Lord (the Covenant): he is their help and their shield.

10. O house of Aaron, trust in the Lord (the Covenant): he is their help and their shield.

11. Ye that fear the Lord (the Covenant) trust in the Lord (the Covenant): he is their help and their shield.

12. The Lord (the Covenant): hath been mindful of us: he will bless us: he will bless the house of Israel; he will bless the house of Aaron.

13. He will bless them that fear the Lord (the Covenant), <u>both small and great.</u>

14. The Lord (the Covenant) shall increase you and more and more, you and your children.

15. Ye are blessed of the Lord (the Covenant) which made heaven and earth.

16. The heaven even the heavens, are the Lords (the Covenant) but the earth hath he given to the children of men.

17. The dead praise not the Lord (the Covenant), neither any that go down into silence.

18. But we will bless the Lord (the Covenant) from this time forth and for evermore. Praise the Lord (the Covenant).

CHAPTER 3

Stop hate, it is the killer of mankind

From my point of view what I am looking at as a spiritual person and of having a good understanding of the words of G_D, it looks like a nonbeliever or atheist have a better chance of going to heaven then a person that goes to church and prays to the image of another man's blood line, and a image of a former slave master every time the door of the church is open. Then when you pray in your mines eyes you see that same image, I say this because you have the word right in front of you and don't study it for yourselves; you set there and let someone tell you his or her view of the bible. But the bible is a book that simply tells us how may time religion has got in the way of mankind, and held him back from seeing the truth. And we as a people still let it get in the way of that truth!

And we have the skills but we don't have the faith in ourselves and the faith that we say G_D give us. We must be afraid of being successful as a people because G_D said that we have been given everything we need to become what he created us for. If you speak the words and believe in your hearts that it will be, and have no doubt in your hearts then what you ask for will come to you. If you only believe and not faint, well as a people we have done a lot of fainting just look at our family life and community life. But we have that lack of faith we would steal from the slave Masters and not want to have anything for ourselves it's a lot better to take from them and we can blame them because we don't believe in ourselves. So we take the lazy way out and we teach our children to take the easy way out and blame whites and teach our children that it is because the white man will not let us have anything for ourselves so why try. Let the white man do it for you, just get a good education and get a good job working for him. Just like the Jewish people of the time of The Prophet Jesus how the Jewish people had given the Rome all the Authority, they the Jewish people where just satisfied with going to the temple and rituals, festivals and the power of the roman government controlled the rest of their life as to who will live and who will die. Because of this I can say to you black man you have eyes and can't see, you have a mouth and can't speak, ears and can't hear, and you have faith and can't use it. Then you Blackman are the fool, and full of no faith in yourselves and the children that you produce, and the future that has been given to you or in the person that you pray to and worship.

But we will not ask ourselves how did the Jewish people get out of their self hate, that the Roman government and the roman church had on them, we act like there is no way out of the condition that we find ourselves in and we go to church every time to doors open but we will not read the words. Then to the person that is entrusted to deliver understanding of G_Ds word he has to know what the word of G_D is saying to mankind. And dig and dig for the truth, it is right in your face and cannot see it because you don't want to see the truth why because you have become dependent on doing nothing for yourself. Now why do white America have so many blessing well it is because they have taken the path of the Pharaohs, and made themselves as a G_Ds for you to worship, so therefore they feel that they are better then you, this is the birth of white supremacy when you make yourselves as a G_D and in all of the religious literature they have their image, and even the watch tower you only see the image of white folk. And they don't want to mix with you, but we have become beggars and very good and we tell our white friends how bad the self hate is and put down our own friends and family with self hate, then you go to church and you pray to the image of the white G_D you can't see the sin of self hate because that is your G_D. and there is none other, so you feel complete.

And at the time of Moses and the relationship with the Jewish people how he Moses had to separate the Jewish People from the ruling class at that time, because man had set himself up as a G_D again and you can see that this is a method of worship that your creator disagrees with, Just take a look at the history, it will tell you that religion was created to separate any people from the way of the Covenant. Just like at the time of Abraham and his people, here again we have that problem of religion getting in the way of the Covenant of the creator. We are like sheep without a Sheppard. A people without a leader without mother or a farther just orphaned and having no direction in their life and under the influences of another man made religion. And we are very comfortable with the religion of a man made religion and the image of another people as your lord.

Psalm 111 1:10

The beginning of wisdom

1. Praise you the Lord (the Covenant). I will praise the Lord (the Covenant) with my whole heart, in the assembly of the upright and in congregation.

2. The works of the Lord (the Covenant) are great, sought out of all them that have pleasure therein.

3. His work is Honorable and glorious: and his righteousness endures forever.

4. He hath made his wonderful works to be remembered the Lord (the Covenant) is gracious and full of compassion.

5. He has given meat unto them that fear him: he will ever be mindful of his Covenant.

6. He has showed his people the power of his works, that he may give them the heritage of the heathen.

7. The works of his hands are verity and judgment; all his commandments are sure.

8. They stand fast forever and ever, and are done in truth and uprightness.

9. He sent redemption unto to his people: he has commanded his Covenant for ever: holy and reverend is his name.

10. The fear of the Lord (the Covenant) is the beginning of wisdom: and good understanding have all they that do his commandments: his praise endures for ever.

CHAPTER 4

Fulfilling the law of Christ (the Covenant)

Now the subject of self hate has a long history it go all the way back to the beginning where man was not happy with the gift of life and the breath of life, He wanted more even before he had a ideal of all he did own. But that kinds of thinking always have been the end of man demise, we always want more then we can bear. Then we head for trouble and the doing harm to something or someone just so we get whatever we need it don't matter what the boundary's are if we want it we have a tendencies to force ourselves on everyone or anyone to get what we need. Regardless of the pain and sorrow and the effect on the condition that are altered on the other person or the object, and that object has been change forever and it state of mine or its form has been altered. But someone knows what form the object was before it was change out of its original stage! may have the decency to return it back to its original state of mine or from.

Freedom from the false Image

Galatians 5 1:12

1. Stand fast therefore in the Liberty where with (the Covenant) had made us free, and be not entangled again with the yoke of bondage (religion).

2. Behold, I Paul say unto you that if ye be circumcised (altered state of mine), (the Covenant) shall profit you nothing.

3. For I testify again to every man that is circumcised (altered state of mine), that he is a debtor to do the whole law.

4. (The Covenant) is become of no effect unto you, whosoever of you is justified by the law; ye are fallen from grace.

5. For us through the spirit wait for hope of righteousness by faith.

6. For in (the Covenant) neither (unaltered state of mine) nor (altered state of mine); but faith which works by love.

7. Ye did run well; who did hinder you that ye should not obey the truth?

8.   This persuasion comes not of him that call you. (That False Image)

9.   A little leaven leavened the whole lump.

10. I have confidence in you through the Lord (the Covenant) that you will be none otherwise minded; but he that troubles you shall bear his judgment, whosoever he is.

11. And I brethren, if you preach circumcision (alter state of mine), why do I yet suffer persecution? Then is the offence of the cross (graven image) ceased.

12.   I would they were even cut off which trouble you.

This is why I feel that are ancestors wrote these Holy books to warm us about the false worships, of the religions of man, and his desire to control the masses and for man to make himself as a G_D. then if you have a problem with the direction of where I am going with this writing. Just look at the different time that man and kings in the Holy books that shows you all the different times that man and kings have captured country and nation and subjected them to different G_D. Don't just take my word for it ready your history for yourselves, because your very eternal life depends on your belief in the Covenant.

Now think just how long we have been subjected and submerged into this mine set of self hate as a people, and we still circulate this among our communities and the indoctrination (to teach somebody a belief, doctrine, or ideology thoroughly and systematically, especially with the goal of discouraging independent thought or the acceptance of other options) of ourselves with this image, do you think this is a problem for our future development as far as we having the change of doing something collectively as a village. And one human family everybody can work together if we can forget our cultural differences, and stop imposing on one another right. But the Africa American Community has to stop the worshipping, of and remove the image of that White image and the cross or anyone else as an idol from their place of worship.

We are stopping our own selves from being what are ancestors wanted for us as a people, if we come to the right spirit of what we are about and what it will take to be that people. And remove all of the garbage out of the communities and set up a culturally rich community self owned and self respected not for us but for the future generation. You have to be willing to change your own condition or else it will not change, no one else knows your condition like we do. Anyone else wouldn't know where to start but we do, and we can fix it with faith and a long time of working together and working smart all things can be done with faith. Plant that mustard seed!

Now this is scriptural words not my, I am just the messenger of that message; don't get mad at me for saying it. Because it is time to pickup that crown that joins us together as one people, and one mankind, and it is time for the righteous to step up and tell the people that King James has miss informed us? Then make the necessary changes in our beliefs. The prophet Jesus (Peace Be on Him) said as long as I am in the world I am the light of the world! Now sense he has been gone man has set himself up as G_D and he man has put us into deep darkness. Then the next Prophet to receive the Light of truth came to the last Prophet Muhammad (Peace Be on Him) and he was of the same bloodline as the other Prophets. You see the message of the Covenant is to contain the created spirit of ADAM that is his breath of life, or the G_D partial of the creator that we must rekindle in order to return to that family spirit of creation and become that living spirit again and the world will know that G_D can give life and cause a people to die.

CHAPTER 5

(How! self hate can turn, to Self Shame and Self Guilt and then Self weakness)

Now the black preacher! He knows the game of self hate and shame, which will lead to guilt and a spiritual, broke down. They are not as slow as you thank! Because most of them think that they are the chosen ones. They are using their understanding of self hate and shame to control the weak and make you feel bad about not worshipping an image of another man as G_D. He is saying to you that everybody else is worshipping this image as their G_D and they are doing OK so what is your problem. So they teach us if you worship this image you will be a much better person, but your condition will not change but G_D loves you because this person that we worship gave his life for your sins. You must believe this and not doubt. Then the preacher will say to his congregation that you are living in sin! And that the only way out is if you believe in this image because he has paid the price for your sin, and you own him your life and because of this act he is your savior. (But I am saying to you that Pharaohs felt the same way when they made themselves as G_Ds).

So we buy what the preacher is selling and try and make this a untruth a truth, in our daily life regardless of the pain and suffering and the sin that is in the seed of the worshipping of the image of another man, when he the preacher has not educated us to love ourselves first and we, Then automatically we fall into self hate, and the shame, which comes from not believing in your own selves and how to use what (the covenant) has given you as a creature of G_D. Then you develop a spirit of self pity and powerlessness' and you fall into nonbelievers of self. You even begin to thank that G_D don't even like you because of what you see of your condition around as a people and you keep trying to make it work, if he did why do all these bad things keeping happening to us. Then he keeps us from being a people that never have something collectively of this life. And never keep us from being kicked around and being rejected and all the loneliness of being on the bottom of life's letter. Well these are some of the side effects of worshipping the image of another man as G_D. Then you keep listing to the Preacher teach us that ever Sunday and you buy it and the sin and pain and suffering that comes with that level of worshipping. So don't get mad at the preacher he didn't put a gun to your heads, you have to read for yourselves. Then go to a place that is teaching the truth.

You see it comes down to this, which white America has fallen into the same trouble as the Pharaohs did. There ancestor back before the time of King James even then they needed and wanted the same kind of power as the Pharaohs so they made a image like themselves and created this new image and used their self. The people that conquer made an image of their self's as a G_D. Now this is the way that I see this problem, the price for this sin is hard, but it fall's on whoever is guilty of the worshipping of any image of any created thing. This is what is said about a false leader taken from ZACNARIAH 11 15:17 and I relate this to careered Preacher and other African America public servants that our overseers and our consider shepherds,

15 The Lord (the Covenant) said to me further: get yourself the gear of a foolish shepherd. 16 for I am going to rise up in the land a shepherd who will neither miss the lost sheep (people). Nor seek the strayed, nor heal the injured, nor sustain the frail, but will feast on the flesh of the fat ones and tear off hoofs. 17 Oh, the worthless shepherd who abandons the flock! Let a sword descend upon his arm and upon his right eye! His arm shall shrivel up; his right eye shall go blind.

Now what I am saying about the worship of this image and this cross it is what is keeping us as a people under the cures of breaking (the covenant) of the Lord of host the lord of Israel! And these African American leaders and public servants along with the community pastors, that are the shepherd (of the people) and our over the sheep (people). For some reason they cannot see others eating the flesh of our future, and the pass, and the present

Just some other verses that speaks of the leadership! (the African American communities all over the world, and under this Doctrine and this false Image) of Black folks. Read and thank of your condition as a human under the leadership of the Black preachers as the Black shepherds.

Then you will find it in Jeremiah 44 2:8

2. Thus said the Lord (the covenant) of host, the G_D of Israel: you have seen all the disaster that I brought on Jerusalem and on all the towns of Judah. They are a ruin today, (as a people) and no one inhabits them (no leadership),

3. on account of the wicked things they did to vex me, going to make offering in worship of other G_Ds which had not known (because we came out of slavery and under fear of the slave masters image as a religion and unread) neither they nor you nor your fathers.

4. Yet I persistently sent to you all my servants the prophets, to say, "Beg you not to do this abominable thing which I hate,"

5. but they would not listen or give ear, to turn back from their wickedness (the worshipping of the image

of another man as your G_D like Egypt did) and not make offerings to other G_Ds;

6.   So my fierce anger was poured out, and it blazed against the towns of Judah and the streets of Jerusalem. And they became a desolate ruin, (no one to protect them from their enemies and themselves) as they still are today.

7.   And now, thus said the Lord, the G_D of Hosts The G_D of Israel; why are you doing such great harm to yourselves, so that every man and woman, child and infant (We teach are youths to worship this image at a young age) of yours shall be cut off from the midst of Judah, and no remnant shall be left of you?

8.   For you vex me (with the worship of a created image of a man, and a wooden cross) by your deeds, making offering to other G_Ds in the land of Egypt (America) where you have come to sojourn, so that you shall be cut off (from the Covenant) and become a curse and a mockery (no respect) among all the nations of the earth.

Now think about what you just read and look into your mirror, and tell yourselves that you don't understand who these people are in these's verse, who are they talking about? And if you have no ideal then you need not read any more of this chapter.

CHAPTER 6

The greatest schemes of the Satan

*T*his is still a stage that we are playing the part of a fool, or a lost sheep (people), or a people that is bent on the worshipping of another man as G_D as the Hebrews did with the Pharaohs and Moses lead us out of EYGPT, and we have the main part in the play. What other people in the bible would be a better fit for the part of Lazarus, that was of a people that was spiritually dead and Jesus woke him up from a deep spiritual sleep because we where wrapped up in the religion worship of man, and he Jesus freed us with the truth about (the covenant). Or what other people can play or would fit the story of the blind man that Jesus used dirt (and the dirt of the earth which is the origin of mans creation from which he was formed) to heal the blindness of man's eyes, and also with the story of Lazarus and the rich man. Or what other people would fit the story of JOB, no other people on earth has ever lost as much as we and we where a great people at one time, that was a righteous man that lose everything and stayed obedience to G_D and G_D restored him with his blessing again. Or what other people would you choice as an example of being swallow by a whale and use religion as the whale, not to mention that the people that would be best suited to play the people of the prodigal son. There is so many stories that fit the condition of people with the same condition of amnesia that we have as a people that got restored again, and one day I Pray that our creator will have mercy on us as a people and bring us back to are right mines of spiritual faith that we once had as a people!.

So that we can engage life again on a community level, and a global level because it is a great feeling, To see trucks on the highway loaded with produces from your own hard work of doing business around the world importing and exporting your production on a community level, and you can see airplanes land and taking off from the airports bring in produces that you purchased from around the world. Then the food that is grown from your farm land and the meat that you eat at the dinner table that was grown on the farms that we own as a community and how much better it would taste coming of the grill or out of the stove. Then right in your own neighborhoods you can purchase these things that were grown on your farms. And the business would have the name of our ancestor above the doors. Then you would see other ethnic groups utilizing your community with respect to you for have faith in yourselves and stopping the self hate among our own kind and others. Then the jobs that you have created among the people. These are some of the feelings that of social-minded people feel when they buy things that they produced it's a different feeling that we have yet to experience that come to a people that have overcome doing for self. And have created a sure future for themselves as a people. And I am very happy for them but that people shouldn't try to stop another from having the same thing as he has in this world because this world is big enough for everybody to have some land they can call their own, after all it is on loan to everyone but with restriction on how the land is manage.

AL SAFFAT SURAH 37, in which the mysteries of the spiritual world are manifested in different ways, tending to the defeat and of evil is throughout connected with revelation, and here the ranged fight is illustrated by a reference to the angels in heaven and to the earlier Prophets in our earth history, from Noah to Jonah. In chronology, this SURAH belongs to the early middle MAKKAN PERIOD. Summary – Through all the mysteries of the heavens and the earth, there is a sorting out of the evil against the good: their final destinations contrasted Peace and victory came to Noah, Abraham, Moses and Aaron. And ILYAS and LUT, in their conflict with Evil. So was it with Jonah when he glorified (the covenant). But men will not ascribe to (the covenant) what is unworthy of him: (the covenant) Prophets strive for his glory, and shall be victorious (the covenant) is one, the source and centre of all affairs, and we must work in discipline, harmony, and unity to put down evil. The hereafter is sure, when personal responsibility will be enforced. For the true and sincere servants of (the covenant), there will be the highest bliss, unmixed and everlasting: for those who defy (the covenants) Law there will be the deepest enduring misery, which will men choose?

4032.   The three acts in verses are consecutive, as shown by the particle I understand them to mean that angels and good men are ever ready to range themselves in ranks in the service of (the covenant) and work in perfect discipline and accord at all times; that they check and frustrate evil wherever they find it and they are strengthened in doing so by their ranging themselves in rank; and that this service furthers the kingdom of (the covenant) and proclaims his message and his glory to all creation.

4033.   That divine message is summed up in the gospel of divine unity, on which the greatest emphasis is laid: "Verily verily your G_D is one". It is a fact intimately connected with our own life and destiny. Your Lord is one who cares for you and cherishes you: you are dear to him. And he is one: it is only he that you have to look to, the source of all goodness, love, and power. You are not the sport of many contending. Forces or blind chances. There is complete harmony and unity in heaven and you have to put yourselves into unison with

it-by discipline in ranks, by unity of plan and purpose in repelling evil, and by concerted action in
promoting the kingdom of G_D. Here is the mys-
tery of the manifold variety of creation pointing
to the absolute unity of the creator.

4037.   The heavens typify not only beauty but power.
The good in (the covenants) world is guarded and
protected against every assault of evil. The evil is
not of the heavenly system: it is a thing in out-
lawry, merely a self-willed rebellion-"cast away on
every side, repulsed under a perpetual penalty"

4038.   We can form a mental picture of the court of the
most high, in the highest heaven, conforming to
the highest idea we can form of goodness, beauty,
purity, and grandeur. The exalted assembly of
angels is given some knowledge of the plan and
will of (the Covenant). Is altogether foreign to
such an atmosphere, but is actuated by feelings of
jealousy and curiosity. It tries to approach by
stealth and overhear something from the august
assembly. It is repulsed and pursued by a flaming
fire, of which we can form some ides in our physical world by the piercing trail of a shooting star.

4040.   They are the doubters, the evil ones, the deniers
of (the covenants) grace and mercy, who laugh at
revelation and disbelieve. Are they more impor-

tant to create than the wonderful variety of beings in (the covenants) spacious creation? Do they forget their own lowly state, as having been created from muddy clay?

4042.   It is indeed strange that unregenerate man should forget, on the one hand, his lowly origin, and on the other hand, his high destiny, as conferred upon him by the grace and the mercy of (the covenant). The indictment of him here comprises four counts: they ridicule the teaching of truth; instead of profiting by admonition, they pay no heed; when (the covenant) signs are brought home to them, they ridicule them as much as they ridiculed the teaching of truth: and when they have to acknowledge incontestable facts, they give them false names like "sorcery", which imply fraud or something which has no relation to their life, although the facts touch the inner springs of their life intimately

4043.   Although the hereafter, and the spiritual life of which it is a corollary, are the most solid facts in our intelligent existence, materialists deny them. They cannot believe that they could have any existence beyond the grave still less their ancestors who died ages and ages ago: how could they ever come to life again?

4044.   They are assured that the future life is a solid fact, but that it will be in very different conditions from those they know now. All their present arrogance will have been humbled in the dust. There will be another plane, in which souls will have experiences quite different from those in their probationary life here. In that life the virtues they will count, and the arrogance they hugged will be brought low. 4046. Their spiritual blindness will then leave them. But they will be surprised at the suddenness of their disillusion.

4047.   The Day of Judgment is the day of sorting out. Good and evil will finally be separated, unlike the apparently inexplicable condition in the present probationary life, when they seem to be mixed together. (But they are not mix together; we have to separate ourselves from falsehoods, and begin to love what you are created for and that is the covenant of peace and righteousness)

4049.   The scene here is after judgment. As in earthly tribunal, the prisoner or his advocate is asked why sentence should not be pronounced upon him, so here those who are proved to have been guilty of wrong are allowed to consider if anything or anyone can help them. Then comes the exposure of the misleaders. (With worshipping of other

G_D; and images; that of false doctrine; that can cause one to break the covenant)

4050.   Obviously no one can stand and intercede, for it is a question of personal responsibility for each soul. No one can help another.

4051.   All the previous arrogance of this life will be gone, but they will face each other, and those who were given a false lead, (at the age of youth the false image of G_D was put in place by the family members and your environment) as in the story of Pharaoh who made themselves as G_D.

4053.   But the fact that others mislead, or that evil example is before us, does not justify us in falling from right conduct. Faith should save us from the fall. But if we have ourselves no faith in right-eousness, or a future life, or the reality of (the covenants) law, how can we blame others? The misleaders can well say that you will be judged according to your misdeeds! The responsibility is personal, and cannot be shifted on the other. The other may get a double punishment, for their own evil, and for misleading their weaker brethren. But the weaker brethren cannot go free from responsibility of their own deeds; for evil means a personal rebellion against (the covenant), if we believe in a personal G_D, evil has no authority over us, except insofar as we deliberately choose it.

4054.   (The covenant) decree of justice requires that every soul should taste the consequences of its own sins, and that decree must be fulfilled. No excuses can save. It is only (the covenants) mercy that can save.

4055.   (This verse is for the creator of images and those that act like they are G_D). Further, the misleaders can well urge against those who reproach them for misleading them:"how could you expect anything better from us? You were warned by (the covenants) Message that we were astray".

4056.   Selfish arrogance was the seed of sin and rebellion of Satan; and Pharaoh; It's that kind of arrogance which prevents man from mending his life and conduct. (<u>Because one man will make himself as a G D and subject the weaker man to worship his image or teach that this image dead for the whole world</u>) When he specks of ancestral ways or public opinion, or national honor, he is usually thinking of himself or of a small clique which thrives on injustice. But the recognition of (the covenant), the one true G_D, as the only standard of life and conduct, the Eternal reality, cuts out self, and is therefore disagreeable to sin.

If false G_Ds are imagined, who themselves would have weaknesses that fit in with sin, they give countenance to evils, and it becomes difficult to give them up, unless (the covenants) grace comes to our assistance.

> 4057.   Possessed of an evil spirit, or man. Such was the charge which the unbelievers sometimes leveled as the prophet in the early stages of his preaching.

> 4058.   The message of Peace, so far from being "mad" or in any way peculiar, is eminently conformable to reason and the true facts of nature as created by (the covenant). It is the truth in the purest sense of the term, and confirms the message of all true messengers that ever lived.

> 4059.   Justice demands that those who sow evil should reap the fruit. But the punishment is due to the conduct and not to anything external to them.

(That brings me to the fact that according to the teaching of the bible, it shows that African Americans had nothing to do with the death of the prophet Jesus. So why should I or you feel guilty of that crime my hand and your are clean)?

> 4061.   The reward of the blessed will not be a chance or a fleeting thing. It will follow a firm decree of (the Covenant), on principles that can be known and understood.

4062.   The spiritual delights are figured forth from parallel experiences in our present life, (your good works will be passed forward and always be of your right hand of justice) and follow an ascending order; food and fruits; gardens of bliss, (with all their charm design, greenery birdsongs fountains) The home of happiness and dignity, with congenial company seated on thrones; delicious drinks from crystal springs for social; and the society of companions of the opposite sex, with beauty and charm but none of the grossness too often incidental to such companionship in this life.

4063.   The passing round of the social cup, as in the case of other pleasures, is without any of the drawbacks and evil accompaniments of the pleasures of this world, (no did respect of the other person rights no harms of any) which are taken as typical behaviors. In drink there is no intoxication: in fruit there is no satiety. "With the bread of angels upon which one lives here and grows not sated.

4064.   These three Foote notes, example how important a chaste womanhood is to the covenant of created mankind?

4067.   The companion was a skeptic, who laughed at (discipline) religion (the ways of the Prophets) and a hereafter. How the tables are now turned! The devout man backed up his faith with a good life and is now in bliss: the other was a cynic and made a mess of his life, and is now burning in the fire.

4068.   He is allowed a peep into the state which he so narrowly escaped by the grace of (THE COVENANT).

4069.   And he (Lazarus) gratefully acknowledges his shortcomings: "I (Lazarus)" should have been a sinner just like this, but for the grace of (the covenant)! He sees that if he had erred it would have been no excuse to plead the other man's example. He (Lazarus) had faith and was saved, to walk in the path of the righteousness.

4070.   After he (Lazarus) realizes the great danger from which he narrowly escaped, his joy is so great that he can hardly believe it! Is the danger altogether past now? Are the portals of death closed forever? Is he (Lazarus) safe now from the temptations which will bring him to ruin and punishment?

4071.   The answer is yes. "Beyond the flight of time, beyond the realm of death, there surely is some blessed clime, where life is not a breath!" in the words of Longfellow this was an aspiration on this earth. And the hereafter it is a realization!

You see there are only two kinds of people in the world, even though there are billions of people, how many of them know the ways of (the covenant) and how many only have been educated in religion. The road of sin is crowded,

Because you are in the ways of the prophets and you understand what the message was that they deliver to mankind and then you applied it to your life, as a way of life, and not as a religion because religion is something that man has thought up and patched together for his usage not the creator and most religions are a outward indoctrination of belief.

4079.   But there is always a band of sincere and devoted men who serve (the covenant), and the highest spiritual life is open to them. The argument of the difference between the fates of the righteous and the unrighteous was begun. Here it is rounded off with the same phrase, and now we proceed to take illustrations from the early Prophets.

CHAPTER 7

(Will the real creator please step forward?)

You see from my understanding of the revelations of the words of our ancestors is this, that the TORAH was a book that was given to mankind to get a clear look and understanding at his time line which is a linage of mankind and how the words of the creator shaped his creation with his words of the Covenant. The TORAH contains the five books of MOSE he the creator give MOSES the keys for mankind which was the commandments which was the Covenant and this Covenant was for mankind, and also a path back to mans created self and a template for all! everything else was false. That also means religion because religion has caused the most harm as far as self-hate. Because black people have been carrying this self-hate every sense our ancestor broke the Covenant, and it goes all the way back to EYGPT, and the Pharaohs yes, hey the Pharaohs made a image of himself as a G_D and the people worship his image and look at the self-hate that he caused with ISRAEL because they worshiped the image of another man now look at how the problem they got dealt. And here we are too as black people doing the same thing as the children ISRAEL did back with the Pharaohs. You see the TORAH tell the story of how man made religion has caused man to break his own created COVENANT and man mislead mankind from the path of truth and his created self of righteousness and religion has caused self-hate.

Then if you understand the words of the TORAH you know that religion has done more harm than it has helped for the change among the African American communities. Which came first the TORAH or the BIBLE, we all know that it was the TORAH and that the King James was a copy of the TORAH, the old testaments and then they man added the New Testaments just to say that they had a book that they can call their own. I say that because I have a better understanding of the Covenant because of reading the TORAH then that tells me there is not a thing wrong with the TORAHS revelation.

The New testaments was wrote hundreds of years after JESUS death and put together based on what a few peoples versions where and then they called it the Kings James Versions. Then in that King Version of the new testaments is where we pick up the three G_Ds and they call it the trinity and someone put a image of themselves on to JESUS and give it to mankind, just like the pharaohs of the pass and called it G_D.

And it replaced the TORAH as being the authority. And this bring us to the greatest book of all time this book explains all the books of the creator words because it has explained the name of the last Covenant and how a righteous person the Covenant of PEACE (ISLAM) is to carry himself and how to live as a way of life, and how important prayer is and the number of prayers a day in a day, and how mankind should live together as one HUMAN family and that all created things live buy their Covenant and it give the name of the last Covenant and the important of knowing what the name is of that that last covenant! We have to stop letting what another man damage has done to us, and take back that power and control that we need to build a future for our young children so when they completed College they can come back the their own environment and plant those blessing and pass those bless for our future with faith in PEACE under the guidance of this Covenant. We can ask the Black churches to let us use the money's that they collect on SUNDAY and deposit that money in with other churches, and build and develop economics in our environments for our brighter future for all mankind. Take better care of our poor Become a giving hand, not just a taking hand! Your condition will not change by itself first you must want to change in your heart, and act on the change. Now this is what the words of G_D tell you it is not my words I am just trying to make to clear for you to understand that we have a commitment to our creator as a people as African American and our children as well. So start reading your TORAH is the (WAY) and your QURAN is the (TRUTH) of the Covenant for understanding of the word, that is where your power lies, not in man but in mankind being one under his last COVENANT called PEACE Islam.

SURAH AL NAHL foot note 2129

It states this: that the Covenant which binds us in the spiritual world makes us strong like strands of fluffy cotton spun into a strong thread. It also gives us a sense of security against much evil in this world of (self Hate). It costs a woman much labor and skill to spin good strong yarn (families). She would be foolish to indeed after she has spin such yarn to untwist its constituent strands and break them into flimsy pieces. C-127 SURAH 16 AL NABL 16;101-128 ALLAH (the covenant) truth may come in stages but it gives strength, guidance, and glad tidings and should be held fast when once received. Be not like those who get puffed up with pride in worldly good, and scorn the truth. Enjoy the good things of life, but render thanks to ALLAH (the Covenant) and obey his (LAW'S) be true in faith and proclaim his word with gentle, patient wisdom. For ALLAH (the Covenant) is with those who live in self restraint a pure, good, and righteous life.

Now you cannot say that you believe in Jesus and not understand the power that lives within you, and not be or make the connection that Christ is a name that was given for (the Covenant) at that time period for Jesus to teach to the people of his time. You see everything is under the control of its laws and commands and that same law was used with Moses and other prophets it never changes. And we as people say that we follow Christ and most of us have never taken the time to read his book called the torah, but you are followers. And we live with all this self hate around us in the homes in the work place in the church in the marriages in the movies ever where you look its about self hate. People are not happy and we call ourselves believers after the Christ, and Christ is not with you if you are not within his commandments and don't even know about the Covenant or the name of his Covenant. But you are up to your neck with Religion, Then on top of all that you worship the IMAGE of another man, just like the children of Israel did worship Pharaoh as a G_D. And you say that this is your Christ and his dead was for everybody man we put a lot of power with that image I just hope it hold up for you on judgment day. And our life reflect a life of total darkness black man void of doing for self and a lot of hate for self, and we are away from that Holy light that guide man by the spirit of faith and truth that drive a man to want something for his self, ALLAH (the Covenant) is the name of the last Covenant given to mankind and woman!

SURAH AL BAQARAH 2:27

27. Those who break ALLAH's Covenant after it is ratified, and who sunder what ALLAH (the covenant) has ordered to be joined, and do mischief on earth: these cause loss (only) to themselves.

28. How can ye reject the faith in ALLAH (the covenant)? Seeing that ye were without life, and he give you life;

then will he cause you to die, and will again bring you to life; and again to him will ye return.

SURAH AL BAQARAH 83:84

83. And remember we took a covenant from the children of Israel (to the effect): worship none but ALLAH (the covenant); treat with kindness your parents and kin-dred. And orphans and those in need; Speck fair to people; be steadfast in prayer; and practice regular charity. Then did ye turn back except a few among you, and ye backslide (even now).

84. And remember we took your covenant (to this effect): Shed no blood amongst you, nor turn out your own people from your home: and this ye solemnly ratified and to this ye can bear witness.

SURAH AL BAQARAH 2:120-121

Never will the Jews or the Christians or (Arabia) be satisfied with thee unless thou follow their form of religion (discipline) say the guidance of ALLAH (the covenant) that is the only guid-ance, wert thou to follow their desires after the knowledge which hath reached thee, then would thou find neither protec-tor nor helper against ALLAH (the covenant) 121. Those to whom we have sent the book study it as it should be studied: they are the ones that believe therein: those who reject faith in (the covenant) therein the loss is their own.

C. 48 – If the people of the book (Bible) rely upon Abraham, let them study his history, his posterity included both Israel and Ismail. Abraham was a righteous man of ALLAH (the covenant). A Muslim (righteous man) and so were his children. Abraham and Ismail built the KABA, as the house of ALLAH (the covenant), and purified it (removed all idols), to be a centre of worship for the entire world: for ALLAH (the covenant) is the Lord of all people.

SURAH AL BAQARAH 2:257

257. ALLAH (the covenant) is the protector of those who have faith; from the depths of darkness (African American) he will lead them forth into light. Of those who reject faith the patrons (false images Idol worshipping) are the evil ones: from the light they will lead them forth into the depths of darkness. They will be companions of the fire, to dwell therein (for ever)

SURAH AL ANFAAL 8:51-56

Because of (the deeds) which your (own) hands sent forth: for ALLAH (the Covenant)is never unjust to his servants: 52 "(deeds) after the manner of the people of Pharaoh and of those before them: They rejected the signs of the ALLAH (the Covenant) and ALLAH (the Covenant)punished them for their crimes: for ALLAH (the Covenant) is strict in punishment: 53 Because ALLAH (the Covenant)will never change the grace which he hath bestowed on a people until they change what is in their (own) souls: and verily ALLAH (the Covenant) is he who hears and knows (all things). 54 "(deeds) after the manner of the people of the Pharaoh and those before them" they treated as false the signs of their: so we destroyed them for their crimes, and we drowned the people of Pharaoh" for they were all oppressors and wrongdoers. 55 For the worst of beasts in the sight of ALLAH (the Covenant) are those who reject him they will not believe. 56 They are those with whom thou make a Covenant but they break their Covenant every time, and they have not the fear (of ALLAH (the Covenant)

You see it is a supreme and very hard sin for man to worship the IMAGE of another man it can create white supremacy, or black supremacy even red supremacy. Not even yourselves as a G_DS. We our only a partials of creation of a great universal, COVENANT THAT SUBSTANES all life, and that it has been given the name of this last UNIVERSAL COVENANT IS CALLED ALLAH! AND THE FIRST COVENANT WAS CALLED ADAM!

I would like to return back to the Hebrew bible in PSALMS and I would recommend that you read the whole verse of 119 of PSALMS, but I enjoy what these words bring out from 119:51-64 and remember that the word LORD! Really means COVENANT when reading this book of MOSES. Because it is from the Prophet David his self about his relationship with interacting with the COVENANT in his life and the Love of the laws of the promise of the worshipping of the POWERFUL Covenant, it is the breath of life! to a dead soul that is lost and has become a victim and a person of self-hate.

Though the arrogant have cruelly mocked me, I have not swerved from your teaching. I remember your rules of old, O Lord (the Covenant) and find comfort in them. I am seized with rage because of the wicked that forsake your teaching. (Now this is specking to the black preachers, who teach us as a people to worship this image of a white man which is white supremacy and self-hate) Your laws are a source of strength to me wherever I may dwell. I remember your name at night, O Lord (the Covenant), and obey your teaching. This has been my lot for I have observed your precepts the Lord (the Covenant) is my portion; I have resolved to keep your words. I have implored you with all my heart; have mercy on me, in accordance with your promise. I have considered my ways and turned back to your decrees. I have hurried and not delayed to keep your commandments (Covenant). Though the bonds of the wicked are coiled round me. I have not neglected your teaching. I arise at midnight to praise you for your just rules. I am a companion to all who fear you, to those who keep your precepts. Your steadfast love, O Lord (the Covenant), fills the earth; teach me your laws.

Now too me that said and had a lot of power in his words! About how and when or if you live according to this great COVENANT because it never changes you are the winner in all cases. And who's the fool if you don't.

CPSIA information can be obtained at www.ICGtesting.com
Printed in the USA
BVOW03s1347090514

353025BV00003B/9/P